EMMANUEL JOSEPH

Lead with Your Voice, Mastering Public Speaking, Psychology, and Action-Oriented Leadership

Copyright © 2025 by Emmanuel Joseph

All rights reserved. No part of this publication may be reproduced, stored or transmitted in any form or by any means, electronic, mechanical, photocopying, recording, scanning, or otherwise without written permission from the publisher. It is illegal to copy this book, post it to a website, or distribute it by any other means without permission.

First edition

This book was professionally typeset on Reedsy.
Find out more at reedsy.com

Contents

1	Chapter 1: The Power of Your Voice	1
2	Chapter 2: The Psychology of Communication	3
3	Chapter 3: Building Confidence in Public Speaking	5
4	Chapter 4: Crafting Your Message	7
5	Chapter 5: Engaging Your Audience	8
6	Chapter 6: Mastering the Art of Persuasion	10
7	Chapter 7: Overcoming Public Speaking Challenges	11
8	Chapter 8: The Role of Leadership in Public Speaking	12
9	Chapter 9: Developing Your Personal Speaking Style	13
10	Chapter 10: The Power of Storytelling	15
11	Chapter 11: Using Visual Aids Effectively	16
12	Chapter 12: Practicing Your Presentation	17
13	Chapter 13: Handling Q&A Sessions	19
14	Chapter 14: Managing Your Speaking Career	21
15	Chapter 15: Continuous Improvement	23
16	Chapter 16: The Impact of Technology on Public Speaking	24
17	Chapter 17: Leading with Your Voice	26

1

Chapter 1: The Power of Your Voice

Your voice is more than just a means of communication; it is a powerful tool that can influence, inspire, and lead. Understanding the significance of your voice in public speaking and leadership is the first step towards mastering its potential.

Your voice has the power to evoke emotions, create connections, and drive action. When used effectively, it can captivate an audience, build trust, and establish credibility. A strong and confident voice can inspire others to believe in your vision, take action, and follow your lead. Whether you are addressing a small group or a large audience, your voice is your most valuable asset in conveying your message and achieving your goals.

The power of your voice lies not only in the words you speak but also in how you speak them. The tone, pitch, and pace of your voice can significantly impact how your message is received. A calm and steady voice can convey confidence and authority, while a passionate and dynamic voice can energize and motivate your audience. Understanding the nuances of vocal delivery and how to use them to your advantage is essential for effective public speaking and leadership.

In addition to vocal delivery, nonverbal communication plays a crucial role in the power of your voice. Your body language, facial expressions, and gestures can reinforce or contradict the words you speak. By aligning your nonverbal cues with your message, you can create a more powerful and authentic connection with your audience. Developing a strong and confident speaking presence involves mastering both verbal and nonverbal communication.

Ultimately, the power of your voice is rooted in your authenticity and passion. When you speak from the heart and genuinely believe in your message, your voice becomes a powerful instrument for change. Authenticity resonates with audiences and builds trust, while passion ignites excitement and inspires action. By harnessing the power of your voice, you can become a more effective and impactful leader.

2

Chapter 2: The Psychology of Communication

Effective communication goes beyond words; it involves understanding the psychology behind how people perceive and process information. By delving into the psychological principles of communication, you can enhance your ability to connect with your audience on a deeper level.

One crucial aspect of communication psychology is nonverbal cues. Nonverbal communication, including body language, facial expressions, and gestures, can convey emotions and intentions more powerfully than words alone. Being aware of and intentionally using nonverbal cues can help you build rapport, trust, and credibility with your audience. For example, maintaining eye contact and using open, relaxed body language can signal confidence and engagement.

Another important psychological principle is the role of emotions in communication. Emotions can influence how your message is received and interpreted. Understanding the emotional state of your audience and tailoring your message to evoke the desired emotional response can significantly impact the effectiveness of your communication. For instance, using storytelling and vivid imagery can elicit strong emotions and make your message more memorable and impactful.

The way people process information also plays a crucial role in communication. Cognitive biases, such as confirmation bias and availability heuristic, can affect how people interpret and respond to your message. By understanding these biases, you can craft your message in a way that minimizes misinterpretation and maximizes clarity. Additionally, using repetition and emphasizing key points can help reinforce your message and ensure it is retained by your audience.

Finally, the psychology of communication involves understanding the dynamics of group communication. Different audiences may have varying needs, preferences, and expectations. Adapting your communication style to suit the specific characteristics of your audience can enhance your ability to connect and engage with them. This might involve adjusting the level of formality, the use of jargon, or the pacing of your speech to match the preferences of your audience.

By understanding and applying these psychological principles, you can become a more effective and influential communicator. In the next chapter, we will explore how to build confidence in public speaking, a key ingredient for successful communication and leadership.

3

Chapter 3: Building Confidence in Public Speaking

Confidence is a key ingredient in successful public speaking. Building and maintaining confidence when speaking in front of an audience is essential for delivering your message with poise and assurance.

One effective strategy for building confidence is positive visualization. Before stepping on stage, take a few moments to visualize yourself delivering a successful speech. Imagine the audience responding positively to your message, applauding, and engaging with your content. This mental rehearsal can help reduce anxiety and boost your confidence.

Controlled breathing is another powerful technique for managing nerves and maintaining composure. Deep, steady breaths can help calm your nervous system and provide a sense of control. Practice breathing exercises regularly to build this habit and use it to center yourself before and during your speech.

Practice is also crucial for building confidence. The more you rehearse your speech, the more comfortable and familiar you will become with the content. Practice in front of a mirror, record yourself, or rehearse with a trusted friend or mentor. Seek feedback and make adjustments as needed. The more you practice, the more confident you will feel when it's time to deliver your speech.

Finally, remember that confidence comes from within. Believe in yourself and your message. Remind yourself of your strengths and accomplishments. Focus on the value you are bringing to your audience and the impact you want to make. When you speak with conviction and authenticity, your confidence will shine through, and your audience will be more likely to trust and engage with you.

In the next chapter, we will explore how to craft a compelling message that resonates with your audience.

4

Chapter 4: Crafting Your Message

A compelling message is the backbone of any effective speech. Crafting a message that resonates with your audience involves clarity, structure, and storytelling.

Clarity is crucial for ensuring your message is understood. Avoid jargon and complex language that may confuse your audience. Instead, use simple, concise language that conveys your message clearly. Define your main points and stick to them, avoiding unnecessary tangents that can dilute your message.

Structure is also important for keeping your audience engaged and ensuring your message flows logically. Begin with a strong opening that captures attention and sets the tone for your speech. Use the body of your speech to present your main points, supporting them with evidence and examples. Conclude with a powerful closing that reinforces your message and leaves a lasting impression.

Storytelling is a powerful tool for making your message memorable and impactful. Use anecdotes and examples to illustrate your points and bring your message to life. Stories can evoke emotions and create connections with your audience, making your message more relatable and engaging.

By focusing on clarity, structure, and storytelling, you can craft a compelling message that resonates with your audience and achieves your communication goals.

5

Chapter 5: Engaging Your Audience

Capturing and maintaining the attention of your audience is crucial for effective public speaking. Engaging your audience involves using a variety of techniques to keep them interested and involved.

One effective technique is using humor. A well-placed joke or light-hearted comment can break the ice and create a positive atmosphere. However, be mindful of your audience and ensure your humor is appropriate and inoffensive.

Rhetorical questions are another powerful tool for engaging your audience. Asking thought-provoking questions can stimulate curiosity and encourage your audience to think about your message. It can also create a sense of dialogue, making your audience feel more involved in your presentation.

Incorporating multimedia elements, such as slides, videos, and props, can also enhance your presentation and capture your audience's attention. Visual aids can help illustrate your points and make your message more dynamic and engaging. However, use them sparingly and ensure they complement your message rather than distract from it.

Interactive activities, such as audience participation exercises and Q&A sessions, can also keep your audience engaged. Involving your audience in your presentation can create a sense of connection and make your message more memorable.

By using these techniques, you can create a dynamic and memorable

CHAPTER 5: ENGAGING YOUR AUDIENCE

presentation that keeps your audience engaged from start to finish.

6

Chapter 6: Mastering the Art of Persuasion

Persuasion is a powerful skill that can help you influence and lead others. Mastering the art of persuasion involves understanding and applying the principles of ethos, pathos, and logos.

Ethos refers to the credibility and trustworthiness of the speaker. Building credibility involves demonstrating your expertise, being honest and transparent, and establishing a connection with your audience. When your audience trusts you, they are more likely to be persuaded by your message.

Pathos involves appealing to the emotions of your audience. Emotional appeals can create a strong connection with your audience and make your message more impactful. Use storytelling, vivid imagery, and passionate delivery to evoke emotions and create a sense of urgency and importance.

Logos refers to the logical arguments and evidence that support your message. Presenting clear, well-reasoned arguments and backing them up with evidence can enhance your credibility and persuade your audience. Use facts, statistics, and examples to support your points and make your message more compelling.

By understanding and applying these principles, you can master the art of persuasion and effectively influence your audience to take action.

Chapter 7: Overcoming Public Speaking Challenges

Public speaking comes with its own set of challenges, from handling difficult questions to managing technical difficulties. Overcoming these challenges involves preparation, adaptability, and maintaining composure.

Handling difficult questions requires preparation and confidence. Anticipate potential questions and prepare thoughtful responses. If you encounter a question you cannot answer, be honest and offer to follow up later. Stay calm and composed, and use active listening to understand the question fully before responding.

Managing technical difficulties involves being adaptable and staying calm under pressure. Test your equipment and materials before your presentation to minimize the risk of technical issues. Have a backup plan in case something goes wrong, and be prepared to adapt your presentation if necessary.

Dealing with stage fright is a common challenge for many speakers. Practice relaxation techniques, such as deep breathing and visualization, to manage anxiety. Focus on the value you are bringing to your audience and remind yourself of your strengths and accomplishments.

By preparing for potential challenges and staying adaptable, you can overcome obstacles and deliver a successful presentation.

8

Chapter 8: The Role of Leadership in Public Speaking

Leadership and public speaking go hand in hand. Understanding the role of leadership in public speaking can enhance your ability to inspire and influence others.

Good leaders lead by example. When you speak confidently and authentically, you set a positive example for your audience. Your voice, tone, and body language can convey your leadership qualities and build trust with your audience. Demonstrating integrity, transparency, and empathy in your speech can further strengthen your leadership presence.

Your voice has the power to inspire and motivate others. By sharing your vision and passion, you can ignite excitement and drive action. Use your voice to articulate your goals and inspire others to join you in achieving them. Leading with your voice involves being persuasive, empathetic, and visionary.

The impact of your voice on your ability to lead cannot be overstated. A strong and confident voice can command attention, build credibility, and create a sense of authority. Your voice can also convey empathy and understanding, which are essential qualities of effective leadership. By mastering the use of your voice, you can become a more impactful and influential leader.

9

Chapter 9: Developing Your Personal Speaking Style

Your personal speaking style is what sets you apart from other speakers. Developing your unique speaking style involves finding your voice and experimenting with different delivery techniques.

Finding your voice involves being authentic and true to yourself. Speak from the heart and let your personality shine through. Your audience will appreciate your authenticity and be more likely to connect with you. Embrace your unique qualities and use them to enhance your speaking style.

Experimenting with different delivery techniques can help you find what works best for you. Try varying your tone, pitch, and pace to see how it impacts your message. Use pauses for emphasis and incorporate gestures to reinforce your points. Practice different techniques and seek feedback to refine your speaking style.

Adapting your speaking style to different audiences and situations is also important. Tailor your delivery to suit the preferences and needs of your audience. For example, a more formal and structured style may be appropriate for a professional setting, while a relaxed and conversational style may be better suited for a casual audience. Being adaptable and versatile can enhance your effectiveness as a speaker.

By developing your personal speaking style, you can create a more engaging and memorable experience for your audience.

10

Chapter 10: The Power of Storytelling

Storytelling is a powerful tool for connecting with your audience and making your message memorable. Effective storytelling involves crafting compelling stories that engage and resonate with your audience.

The key elements of effective storytelling include character development, plot structure, and emotional appeal. Characters give your story a human element and make it relatable. Develop your characters by providing details about their background, personality, and motivations.

A well-structured plot keeps your audience engaged and interested. Your story should have a clear beginning, middle, and end. Start with an attention-grabbing opening, build tension and conflict in the middle, and conclude with a satisfying resolution. A well-paced plot keeps your audience on the edge of their seats and eager to hear more.

Emotional appeal is crucial for making your story memorable. Use vivid imagery, sensory details, and emotional language to evoke feelings and create a strong connection with your audience. Share personal anecdotes and experiences to make your story more relatable and impactful.

By mastering the art of storytelling, you can create a more engaging and memorable presentation that leaves a lasting impression on your audience.

11

Chapter 11: Using Visual Aids Effectively

Visual aids can enhance your presentation and help convey your message more effectively. Using visual aids involves selecting and integrating them in a way that supports your message without distracting from your delivery.

When selecting visual aids, consider their relevance and effectiveness in illustrating your points. Choose visual aids that complement your message and enhance understanding. For example, slides, props, and videos can provide visual reinforcement for your key points and make your presentation more dynamic.

Design your visual aids with clarity and simplicity in mind. Avoid cluttered and complex visuals that may confuse your audience. Use clear and concise text, high-quality images, and consistent design elements. Ensure that your visual aids are easy to read and understand from a distance.

Integrate your visual aids seamlessly into your presentation. Practice using them in your rehearsals and ensure they align with your verbal delivery. Use visual aids to highlight key points, provide examples, and reinforce your message. Avoid relying too heavily on visual aids, as your voice and presence should remain the primary focus.

By using visual aids effectively, you can enhance your presentation and create a more engaging and memorable experience for your audience.

12

Chapter 12: Practicing Your Presentation

Practice is essential for mastering public speaking. Effective practice involves rehearsing your presentation, receiving feedback, and making adjustments to improve your performance.

Start by practicing your presentation in front of a mirror or recording yourself. This allows you to observe your body language, facial expressions, and vocal delivery. Take note of areas that need improvement and make adjustments as needed. Repeated practice will help you become more familiar with your content and build confidence.

Seek feedback from trusted friends, mentors, or colleagues. Share your presentation with them and ask for their honest feedback. Listen to their suggestions and make necessary changes. Constructive feedback can provide valuable insights and help you refine your presentation.

Incorporate a variety of practice techniques, such as practicing in different environments, timing yourself, and simulating real-life scenarios. Practice delivering your presentation in front of small groups to build confidence and receive additional feedback. The more you practice, the more comfortable and confident you will become.

Effective practice involves continuous improvement. Regularly review and update your presentation based on feedback and new insights. Stay open to learning and be willing to make adjustments to enhance your performance. By practicing effectively, you can master the art of public speaking and deliver impactful presentations.

13

Chapter 13: Handling Q&A Sessions

Q&A sessions can be a valuable opportunity to engage with your audience and address their concerns. Handling Q&A sessions effectively involves preparation, active listening, and confident responses.

Preparation is key to handling Q&A sessions confidently. Anticipate potential questions related to your topic and prepare thoughtful responses. Have a clear understanding of your main points and be ready to provide additional details and examples. Being well-prepared will help you respond confidently and accurately.

Active listening is crucial during Q&A sessions. Listen carefully to each question and ensure you understand it fully before responding. Paraphrase or repeat the question to confirm your understanding and show that you are actively engaged. Active listening demonstrates respect for your audience and enhances your credibility.

When responding to questions, remain calm and composed. Provide clear and concise answers, and avoid getting defensive or evasive. If you do not know the answer to a question, be honest and offer to follow up later. Acknowledge the question and provide relevant information, even if you cannot answer it fully.

Q&A sessions provide an opportunity to reinforce your message and build rapport with your audience. Use them to address any concerns, clarify misunderstandings, and provide additional insights. By handling Q&A sessions effectively, you can enhance your credibility and create a positive connection with your audience.

14

Chapter 14: Managing Your Speaking Career

Public speaking can be a rewarding career, but it requires careful planning and management. Building a successful speaking career involves marketing yourself, building your brand, and finding speaking opportunities.

Marketing yourself is essential for attracting speaking engagements. Create a professional portfolio that showcases your expertise, experience, and accomplishments. Develop a strong online presence through a personal website and social media platforms. Share valuable content, such as articles, videos, and blog posts, to demonstrate your knowledge and build your reputation.

Building your brand involves establishing a unique identity and positioning yourself as an expert in your field. Define your niche and target audience, and tailor your content and messaging to meet their needs. Develop a consistent and recognizable brand image, including your logo, colors, and tagline. Building a strong brand can help you stand out in a competitive market and attract more speaking opportunities.

Finding speaking opportunities requires proactive effort. Network with other speakers, event organizers, and industry professionals. Attend conferences, workshops, and networking events to connect with potential clients and collaborators. Submit proposals to speak at industry events and reach out to organizations that align with your expertise. Building relationships and staying active in your industry can help you uncover new opportunities.

Managing your time and setting goals are also important for a successful speaking career. Create a plan that outlines your short-term and long-term goals, and develop a schedule to achieve them. Stay organized and prioritize your tasks to ensure you meet deadlines and deliver high-quality presentations. By managing your speaking career effectively, you can achieve long-term success and make a positive impact.

15

Chapter 15: Continuous Improvement

Public speaking is a skill that requires continuous improvement. Ongoing development involves seeking feedback, learning from other speakers, and staying up-to-date with industry trends.

Seek feedback regularly to identify areas for improvement. After each presentation, ask for feedback from your audience, peers, or mentors. Listen to their suggestions and reflect on your performance. Use this feedback to make necessary adjustments and enhance your skills.

Learn from other speakers by observing their techniques and styles. Attend conferences, watch TED Talks, and listen to podcasts to gain insights from experienced speakers. Take note of what works well and incorporate those techniques into your own presentations. Learning from others can provide valuable inspiration and help you refine your speaking style.

Stay up-to-date with industry trends and best practices. Read books, articles, and research papers on public speaking and leadership. Participate in professional development courses and workshops to enhance your knowledge and skills. Staying informed about the latest trends can help you stay relevant and deliver impactful presentations.

Continuous improvement requires a growth mindset and a commitment to learning. Embrace challenges, be open to feedback, and stay motivated to become the best speaker you can be. By continuously improving your skills, you can achieve long-term success and make a lasting impact.

16

Chapter 16: The Impact of Technology on Public Speaking

Technology has transformed the way we communicate and present information. Understanding the impact of technology on public speaking can help you leverage digital tools to enhance your presentations and reach a wider audience.

Virtual presentations have become increasingly popular, allowing speakers to connect with audiences from around the world. Familiarize yourself with virtual presentation platforms, such as Zoom, Microsoft Teams, and Webex. Learn how to use these platforms effectively, including features like screen sharing, breakout rooms, and interactive polls. Practicing virtual presentations can help you build confidence and deliver engaging content online.

Social media is another powerful tool for public speakers. Platforms like LinkedIn, Twitter, and Instagram can help you promote your speaking engagements, share valuable content, and connect with your audience. Use social media to build your brand, engage with your followers, and create a community around your expertise. Consistent and strategic use of social media can help you reach a wider audience and establish yourself as a thought leader.

Digital tools, such as presentation software, design apps, and audience engagement platforms, can enhance your presentations. Tools like PowerPoint, Canva, and Prezi can help you create visually appealing slides and graphics. Audience engagement platforms like Mentimeter and Slido can facilitate interactive activities and real-time feedback. Leveraging these tools can make your presentations more dynamic and impactful.

By embracing technology and incorporating digital tools into your presentations, you can enhance your communication skills and connect with a broader audience.

17

Chapter 17: Leading with Your Voice

In the final chapter, we bring together the concepts discussed throughout the book and focus on leading with your voice. Using your voice to inspire, influence, and create positive change is the ultimate goal of mastering public speaking, psychology, and action-oriented leadership.

Leading with your voice involves being authentic and speaking from the heart. When you genuinely believe in your message and communicate with passion and conviction, your voice becomes a powerful instrument for change. Authenticity resonates with audiences and builds trust, while passion ignites excitement and inspires action.

Incorporate the principles of effective communication, including clarity, structure, storytelling, and persuasion, to enhance your message. Use your voice to articulate your vision, share your goals, and motivate others to join you in achieving them. Your voice can create a sense of purpose and direction, driving others to take action and make a positive impact.

Empathy and understanding are also essential qualities of effective leadership. Use your voice to listen, connect, and address the needs and concerns of your audience. Show empathy by acknowledging their experiences and providing support and encouragement. Leading with empathy can foster collaboration, build strong relationships, and create a positive and inclusive environment.

By mastering the skills of public speaking, psychology, and action-oriented

CHAPTER 17: LEADING WITH YOUR VOICE

leadership, you can lead with confidence and make a lasting impact. Use your voice to inspire, influence, and create positive change in your organization and community.

Title: Lead with Your Voice: Mastering Public Speaking, Psychology, and Action-Oriented Leadership

Description: "Lead with Your Voice" is a comprehensive guide designed to help you master the art of public speaking, understand the psychology behind effective communication, and develop action-oriented leadership skills. This book is your roadmap to becoming a more confident and impactful speaker and leader.

In this book, you'll discover the power of your voice and how it can influence, inspire, and lead others. You'll delve into the psychology of communication, learning how nonverbal cues, emotions, and cognitive biases shape the way people perceive your message. With practical strategies for building confidence, crafting compelling messages, and engaging your audience, you'll be equipped to deliver powerful presentations that leave a lasting impact.

The book also explores the art of persuasion, offering techniques to build credibility, evoke emotions, and present logical arguments that drive action. You'll learn how to overcome common public speaking challenges, handle difficult questions, and adapt to unexpected situations with poise and assurance.

Leadership plays a central role in this guide, highlighting the qualities of a good leader and the importance of leading by example. You'll develop your personal speaking style, harness the power of storytelling, and use visual aids effectively to enhance your presentations.

With chapters dedicated to managing your speaking career, seeking continuous improvement, and leveraging technology, this book provides a holistic approach to public speaking and leadership. By leading with your voice, you can inspire, influence, and create positive change in your organization and community.

www.ingramcontent.com/pod-product-compliance
Lightning Source LLC
LaVergne TN
LVHW020742090526
838202LV00057BA/6181